Published by Sweet Cherry Publishing Limited
Unit 36, Vulcan House,
Vulcan Road,
Leicester, LE5 3EF
United Kingdom

First published in the US in 2022
2022 edition

2 4 6 8 10 9 7 5 3 1

ISBN: 978-1-80263-044-2

© Harry Meredith

Soccer Rising Stars: Phil Foden

Cover design and illustrations
by Sophie Jones

Lexile® code numerical measure L – Lexile® 890L

www.sweetcherrypublishing.com

Printed and bound in Turkey

SOCCER RISING STARS

PHIL FODEN

THE UNOFFICIAL STORY

Written by
HARRY MEREDITH

Sweet Cherry

CONTENTS

VIRTUOSO

On the 7th of February 2021, Manchester City were facing one of their toughest matches of the season. The team had traveled to Anfield, home of Liverpool FC, who were the reigning champions of the Premier League. Although the Premier League trophy wouldn't be decided on this

occasion, the victor would take a crucial step in the right direction. The City squad knew that Liverpool were not going to give up their title without a fight.

Manchester City had not won an away game at Anfield in eighteen years. If they wanted to break this cycle, then the players would need to perform at their absolute best. The Manchester squad emerged from the tunnel with complete focus. Adrenaline surged through their veins. But as the players stepped out onto the field they were greeted by silence.

Due to the COVID-19 pandemic, fans were not allowed at the match. The chanting of home fans in the famous Kop stand, which created such an electric atmosphere in normal times, would not play a part in this game. Despite this, the tension and history of the fixture still weighed on the players' shoulders. For every player on the field, pride was at stake as well as points. Could this Manchester City team finally break their Anfield curse?

Leading the line for Manchester City was Phil Foden. The talented player, developed through City's own

academy, was going to do everything he could to make sure his team won the match. In previous seasons, Phil had played a supporting role for the team. For most of his appearances, he had came off the bench as a substitute. But during this season, Phil was turning into a leading man. He was a star player who could instantly change a game.

The referee brought the whistle to his mouth and the game kicked off. Neither team wanted to allow a goal early on, so both sides were cautious

at the start. But as the minutes in the first half began to tick by, chances started to appear. In the 37th minute, Manchester City sprang into Liverpool's half. Raheem Sterling, the nippy winger, burst into the penalty area and tried to wriggle his way through the Liverpool defense. But as he did, a Liverpool defender tripped him, causing Sterling to fall to the ground. *Penalty!* The referee awarded a spot kick and İlkay Gündoğan stepped up to take it.

In previous fixtures, Manchester City had bad luck with penalties.

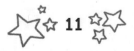

Phil and the rest of the team looked on in hope as Gündoğan ran up to the ball. In the silent stadium, Phil prayed for a goal. But as the ball left Gündoğan's boot, it flew over the crossbar. Manchester City's poor run of penalties continued.

Shortly after, the halftime whistle was blown and the teams headed into their dressing rooms. Despite the missed penalty, Manchester City were in good spirits. They'd put on a strong performance. If they could push just that little bit harder, then three points

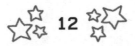

were there for the taking. After Pep Guardiola's team talk, Phil stood up from his bench.

"Can I speak, coach?" asked Phil.

"Go ahead," said Guardiola, surprised by the midfielder's request.

"We're in control of this match. We might be at their ground, but don't forget where we are in the table. We're in top spot for a reason. Any field in this country is ours if we want it. Let's do it, lads!"

The players cheered, and Guardiola couldn't help but smile. "Well said, Phil. Let's go!"

The City players returned for the second half with a newfound confidence, and it showed on the field. In the 49th minute, Phil pounced on a loose pass by Liverpool's Trent Alexander-Arnold. He danced his way around the defense before prodding the ball to Sterling. Sterling drove into the box and passed the ball back to Phil.

Only a couple of meters away from goal, there was only one thought on Phil's mind: *shoot!* The ball stung the gloves of Liverpool's goalkeeper, Alisson, but he was unable to gather it in time. It rebounded into the penalty area and Gündoğan ran onto the loose ball. Gündoğan fired the ball at the goal, desperate to make amends for his penalty miss. He wasn't going to miss this time. *Goal!* Manchester City had the lead.

Falling behind had ignited a fire in the Liverpool squad. They created more chances and earned a penalty as Mohamed Salah was brought down in the box by Rúben Dias. The Liverpool star tucked his penalty away with ease, and the rest of the Liverpool team cheered in delight. It was level at 1-1.

The Liverpool goalkeeper made an unforced error as he tried to clear the ball in the 73rd minute. Instead of finding a player in red, the ball fell to Phil! He brought the ball under his control and charged into the penalty area. He was too far to the side to shoot, so he passed the ball across the box for Gündoğan to tap in. *Goal!* City were in the lead again.

Not long after that, the game turned from bad to horrific for the Liverpool goalkeeper. Once more, Alisson gave the ball away and Manchester City seized the chance. This time, Bernardo

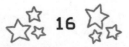

Silva chipped the ball to the back post where Sterling scored with a diving header. Manchester City now had a comfortable lead with the match at 1-3. But the best goal of the game was still to come.

In the 83rd minute, Gabriel Jesus played a cross-field pass to Phil. He controlled the ball on the right wing and dribbled into the opposition box. Before a defender could stop him, Phil pulled back his left foot and unleashed a rocket. The ball flew over Alisson's head, moving so fast that he hardly had the time to raise his hands. *Goal!*

The ball struck the back of the net and Phil's teammates surrounded him in celebration.

A smile beamed from Phil's face as the referee blew the final whistle. Manchester City had held on to their lead. Their Anfield curse was over, and Phil had just played one of his best games for the club. The young star, who'd had to wait in line behind so many talented players, was proving why he was at this club. He had shown the world that he deserved his place in a lineup of players worth hundreds of millions of dollars.

This Manchester-born lad, who loved his club to the core, was going to do far more than just make the starting eleven. Phil was a star in the making, and no one was going to stop him from taking the soccer world by storm.

FROM CRIB TO CONTRACT

Phil was born on the 28th of May 2000. He grew up in a loving home in Edgeley, a suburb of Stockport. While the world knows him as Phil, his family often call him "Ronnie".

His father is also called Phil, so to
avoid confusion the young boy was
given the nickname Ronnie by his
grandmother. While Phil grew up
in an area that wasn't so well off,
he enjoyed a happy childhood. The
neighborhood may not have had
million-dollar soccer fields, but there
was something that it cherished above
all: soccer.

The Foden family loved the game.
This passion quickly rubbed off on

 Phil. His parents even
placed a toy ball in his crib
as a baby, and it quickly

became his favorite toy to play with.

Soft toys were soon replaced with mini soccer balls, and Phil began dribbling around the house and kicking the ball against the furniture—when his mom wasn't looking of course! As he was always playing soccer, his natural abilities were clear for everyone to see. At just 4 years old, Phil was put on Manchester City's radar thanks to a tip from their local scouting network. But as he was too young to sign with the club, Phil eventually registered with a local team called the Reddish Vulcans.

Starting at the Vulcans as a 6-year-old, Phil was easily the best player in the team and against any opposition they faced. Phil was so good that even the parents of players on rival teams could do nothing but gasp, stare and clap in awe at his talent. Some said that he was so good they should be paying to watch him.

After matches with the Vulcans, scouts from other professional teams lined up to have a word with Phil's father. They tried to get him to consider sending Phil to their soccer academies once he was old enough.

 But there was only ever going to be one academy he would consider for his son. Phil enjoyed a two-year stay with the Vulcans before his journey in the sky blue of Manchester City began.

At the age of 8, Phil trained with mixed age groups a couple of nights a week. Despite being a small player and being born later in the school year, his strength was never a concern. Phil's greatest asset was that no player could ever take the ball from him. No matter how strong or tall they were,

Phil always found a way to get past the opposition and protect the ball.

Phil officially signed with Manchester City's academy as a 9-year-old. The club would have signed him much earlier, but they weren't legally allowed to. Once Phil's junior contract had been signed, there were smiles all around in the head office of the coaches and staff. They believed that they were now coaching one of the best soccer talents in the entire country.

But Phil's development was only just beginning. At this stage of his

career, there were hundreds of young
players on the fields at the academy. In
teams of different age groups, young
hopefuls were giving their all to be the
player who made it to the top. Yet even
in those talented crowds, academy
staff were drawn to the matches
Phil was playing in. His enormous
potential was clear to see.

When playing in a local tournament,
it looked as though Phil had the ball
stuck to his feet. He dribbled past
the opposition's midfield, keeping
the ball close to him at all times. Phil
pretended to pass before pushing the

ball past the fooled defender, leaving him rooted to the ground with no choice but to watch Phil sail past. An onrushing goalkeeper dove at his feet, but Phil rolled the ball away from his

outstretched arms. Two defenders came off the goal line, trying to stop Phil's charge. Phil swept past the first defender with ease, before delicately dinking the ball past the last defender and into the net.

The young star turned, celebrated and immediately ran back into his

own half to get ready to do it all over again. It wasn't a question of *if* Phil would make it as a professional for Manchester City. It was a question of *when*.

3
MIRACLE MATCH

Although Phil spent the majority of his week playing soccer at the academy, he always found time for his friends Mike, Jake and Alan. He'd often play street soccer with them on the pavements and roads outside of their houses. With the street being narrow

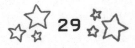

and tucked away, cars rarely traveled through it. However, the boys always had to keep an eye out for cars as playing on any road can be dangerous.

"I'm free!" called Phil.

Mike passed him the ball and Phil controlled it with ease. Jake and Alan on the other side looked at one another and sighed. They knew it was nearly impossible to take the ball from Phil. Jake dashed toward him, but Phil rolled the ball to the right. By the time Jake got to him, Phil was a meter to the side. With determination, Alan charged, but Phil never panicked.

He slotted the ball through Alan's legs and sprang aside, turning as he did to avoid his onrushing friend.

Phil dribbled over to the makeshift goal and passed the ball for Mike to score. But his friend's shot cannoned into the air off a curb. It was too far away for the boys to catch it. Instead of into their arms, the ball soared toward a parked car. The boys could do nothing as it fell from the sky and bounced on the hood. They gritted their teeth as the car's lights began to flash. The car's alarm pierced the ears of every resident on the street.

But before the car's owner could peel back their living room curtains, Phil and his friends had already darted into his house to hide.

Later that day (and after an apology to the unhappy neighbor!), Phil headed to watch one of the most exciting soccer matches in Premier League history. He and his mom had tickets to watch Manchester City vs Queens Park Rangers at the Etihad stadium.

It was the last day of the 2011/2012 season. With the two teams usually fighting at opposite ends of the league table and not a direct threat to each other, this fixture was far more important than it would typically be. Manchester City were top of the table. If they could equal or better the result of their fierce rivals Manchester United, they'd be crowned champions of the Premier League. But the rivalries didn't end there. While Phil and his mom were going to the City match, Phil's dad certainly wasn't. He was a Manchester United fan!

Phil's team were only one match away from title glory and he wasn't going to miss it. He arrived with

his mom at a stadium exploding with tension and excitement. The Premier League trophy was heading to Manchester by the end of the night. But would it be decorated in the red of Manchester United or in the sky blue of Manchester City?

City started well and scored the first goal of the match in the 39th minute. QPR goalkeeper Paddy Kenny was unable to keep Pablo Zabaleta's strike from crossing the line. But QPR had something to fight for too. They needed more points than their nearest rivals to avoid relegation to the

Championship league. They refused to go down easily.

Djibril Cissé scored in the 48th minute and the game was level at 1-1. Only a handful of minutes later, QPR midfielder Joey Barton received a red card for elbowing Carlos Tevez and was sent off. Surely with one man more than QPR the match was Manchester City's for the taking? But QPR's reduced ten-man squad shocked everyone by taking the lead

 in the 66th minute. Jamie Mackie's header bounced on the ground before

passing the outstretched arms of City goalkeeper Joe Hart.

Nervous City fans in the stands got to their feet in a panic and blocked Phil's view. Phil climbed onto his seat to try to see the field over them. He overheard from one of the fans that Manchester United were winning their match elsewhere. Now Manchester City needed to score not just once but twice more to clinch the title.

Time quickly passed by and City fans' hopes began to fade. Before Phil knew it, the ninety minutes of game time had passed and City still trailed 1-2. The fourth assistant held up the electrical board—there were five minutes of extra time. But surely it was too late now? Phil wasn't going to give up hope. He crossed his fingers on both hands and nudged his mother's arm.

"You too, Mom," he said, and she crossed her fingers too.

After two minutes of the additional five, Manchester City had a corner. David Silva whipped in a cross and Edin Džeko rose highest to meet it. He headed the ball into the back of the net and the stadium erupted.

Manchester City had a chance! There were three more minutes to play. The City players ran back into position on a wave of hope. Could they achieve the impossible?

Play restarted and an exhausted QPR side booted the ball away. They just wanted the match to be over to avoid relegation to a lower league. But Manchester City *needed* a goal—just one more to be crowned champions. Just one more goal to achieve soccer immortality.

Sergio Agüero fed the ball to Mario Balotelli on the edge of the box.

Balotelli held off an approaching defender and played it back to Agüero. The Argentinian striker made his way into the penalty box and tried to create an opportunity. He pulled back his right foot and took his shot …

Goal!

Manchester City had done it. Phil's mom picked him up and hugged him. Phil looked across the stands and saw thousands upon thousands of fans smiling, crying and singing together. It was an incredible feeling. He'd witnessed his heroes perform a miracle. This was his club, and he

hoped that one day he could be a player on that field. He wanted to be the one twirling his shirt around in his hand in celebration and leading the club to a Premier League trophy.

4

MANCHESTER CITY ACADEMY

At the age of 10, Phil was playing for the academy side in a match against Middlesbrough. Without breaking a sweat, Phil had played his part scoring a whopping five out of City's

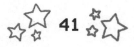

ten goals against decent opposition. Middlesbrough's academy was made up of talented young players who had been scouted. They just couldn't compete with Phil's talent.

On a nearby field, Manchester City's under 14s were also playing against Middlesbrough's. At halftime, the coaches of City's U10 and U14 sides came together to chat. The U10s coach glanced over at Phil before nodding at his colleague and walking over to Phil.

"You're doing great," he said. "Almost too great!"

"Thanks," laughed Phil.

"I've spoken to our other coach and we've had an idea. How about we put you in the U14 game for the second half and give you a real challenge?"

Phil grinned. "I'm ready," he said.

Phil joined up with the older boys and it was a harsh test. The players were much taller, stronger and more experienced than Phil. But Phil didn't let this faze him. He played the same confident game he always did. Parents and onlookers across the site were slowly drawn to the field. Everyone wanted to watch Phil.

To the amazement of everyone watching, Phil scored the winning goal of the match to make the score 2-1. He met a cross with a diving header and the goalkeeper could do nothing but watch as it rocketed into the net. No matter what age group Phil was playing in, he only excelled.

Phil powered through every training session. He wasn't going to let his opportunity with City pass him by. As the years at the academy passed, nothing ever changed in Phil's attitude or approach. He was going to make it. No matter what, he was going to become a professional soccer player.

Every now and then at the academy complex, Phil would see one of his heroes in a corridor. Other times he would walk past a training field where they were practicing for their next big game. No matter how frequent these sightings were, Phil always felt the same excitement. If he could keep on going, he hoped that in a few years he'd be playing on the field with them. Then one afternoon, instead of walking past Phil, one of his favorite players stopped in a corridor and nodded at him.

"Hello, mate," said the player.

Phil stood there with his mouth wide open. He took a second to compose himself and find the words to reply.

"H-hello," said Phil. Towering above him was Vincent Kompany—the team's captain. He was a role model for the players around him as much as he was for the fans who supported the team. The gigantic center-back couldn't help but grin at Phil's reaction.

"I saw you on one of the fields today. You did really well. What's your name?"

"Phil Foden," Phil managed to utter.

"I'll make sure to remember that," said Kompany. "Keep up the good work. You've got talent."

As Kompany walked down the corridor, Phil stood awestruck. The first-team captain had told him he was talented! Phil couldn't stop smiling for an entire week.

5
CAREER CROSSROADS

Phil rose through the academy year
groups and at the age of 16 was
getting closer and closer to first-team
soccer. Players at this age often start
to consider their route into the first
team. In fact, some talented players are
already involved with the first team

at 16 years old. But Phil's situation was less simple. While he was an incredible talent, Manchester City was overflowing with talented players who were also fighting for a spot on the first team. The club was also experiencing its best ever run of form.

Following the purchase of the club by Sheikh Mansour, money had been poured into the club. The wealthy chairman had invested millions of dollars. For the club's fans this was brilliant, as they were likely to experience more success and see incredible

new players bought for the team. But this also meant that the route to the first team narrowed for local talent. In order to make it into a first-team squad overflowing with star players, academy players needed to be among the best in the world. But Phil was no ordinary talent. If any academy player could make it at Manchester City, it was him.

Nevertheless, the competition was fierce. Manchester City also had the likes of Jadon Sancho and Brahim Díaz on their books: two attacking starlets who were showing great potential.

These two tricksters often pulled off dazzling moves and wowed spectators. Phil was always seen as talented, but he didn't play with the same flair that they did. This meant that he could sometimes be overlooked. But for those who watched him match after match, one thing was clear:

Phil Foden was a superstar.

One lunch after a tough training session, Phil and Díaz were sitting down at the cafeteria table. A huge mound of pesto pasta covered Phil's plate. Phil glanced at his phone, blowing on his hot meal.

"I wonder where Jadon's at?" he said.

"Probably fallen asleep watching videos of Ronaldinho," said Díaz.

"That sounds about right," said Phil, tucking into his pasta.

A few minutes later, Sancho walked into the cafeteria. He was wearing jeans and a polo shirt instead of his usual training gear. He pulled up a chair next to his friends and nabbed a sweet potato fry from Díaz's plate.

"Oi!" said Díaz.

"Too slow," Sancho grinned.

"Where have you been?" asked Phil. "And where's your uniform?"

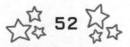

"Well," Sancho began, "I wanted to tell you guys first."

He looked around to make sure no one else was listening.

"You know I told you guys a club was interested in me? Well they've agreed a fee. I've signed for Borussia Dortmund."

Phil and Díaz congratulated their friend, but at the same time they were sad to see him go. The three of them were incredibly talented soccer players, and in many clubs they would have already slotted into the first team. But at Manchester City that

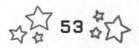

journey was tough given the club's depth of talent.

Sancho had made the hard decision to leave, and this played on Phil's mind. Was he doing the right thing staying at Manchester City? To give himself some room to think, Phil planned to spend the weekend as far away from the soccer field as possible.

★ ★ ★

Ever since he was little, Phil had loved fishing. Whenever he got a chance, he would set off with his father to clear his mind and cast his rod. One weekend, after Sancho's announcement, Phil was sitting peacefully by the water waiting for his line to pull. With the morning sun in the sky, Phil and his father basked in the warmth.

"Do you think I should stay at City?" asked Phil.

"What I think is that you should be quiet. Can't have you scaring all the bleedin' fish away," said his father.

Phil laughed and gave him a nudge.

"Honestly, if you're happy, then I see no reason to move," said his father.

Phil looked at his fishing rod, waiting patiently.

"I am happy there," said Phil. "It's just seeing Jadon's opportunity at Borussia

Dortmund ..."

"That might be right for him," said Phil's father, "but it doesn't mean it's right for you. Just bide your time. I know, and you know, that you're brilliant. Your time with the first team will come sooner or later."

Time ticked by and Phil still hadn't caught a bite. But sitting on his camping chair, staring out over

the water, Phil didn't really care. He was just happy to be in the moment, enjoying his favorite hobby with his dad. He was patient, and it was then that his line tightened, as ripples formed on the surface of the water. At last: a bite.

6

PRESEASON IN THE USA

In preparation for the 2017/2018
Premier League campaign, the City
players returned for pre-season
training. The first-team players had
come back from their vacations only to

quickly be sent off on another flight: they had been invited to play in a pre-season tournament in the USA.

As an academy player, Phil expected to continue his pre-season training in Manchester. However, Phil and three of his academy teammates were taken aside from their group one morning. The academy coach led the four of them back outside the training complex. Phil and Díaz, along with Daniel Grimshaw and Arijanet Muric, had no idea what was going on. Their coach's expression was hard to read.

"What have we done?" asked Grimshaw. "Are we in trouble?"

"Far from it, lads," said the coach, finally breaking into a smile. "On our recommendation, the four of you will not be carrying out pre-season training at the complex. You're all joining up with the first team and heading off to the USA."

The four teammates gaped at one another in shock before breaking into smiles and laughter. Phil could hardly contain his excitement. This was an incredible opportunity. He had a

chance to show the manager just what he could do. This was his chance to break through.

Phil traveled with the team to the USA and trained with the team's superstars. He couldn't quite get used to playing one-twos with Kevin De Bruyne every morning, or practicing shooting with the likes of Agüero. What Phil hadn't noticed during these training sessions was that the manager, Guardiola, was keeping an eye on him. Guardiola liked what he had seen and decided that Phil was going to play in the first match of the

pre-season tournament: a not-so-friendly encounter against the club's biggest rivals—Manchester United.

The players emerged from the tunnel to smoke machines and stage lights. This was nothing like what Phil was used to back in England. The teams went onto the field as if they were participating in the Super Bowl. Music blared from the stadium speakers and there was a light show not too different from a school disco.

Phil put on an impressive performance, but the team suffered a 2-0 loss.

Goals from Romelu Lukaku and Marcus Rashford won the match for Manchester United.

Next up was a trip to Los Angeles, where Manchester City would take on Real Madrid. Playing against a team with the likes of Cristiano Ronaldo, Karim Benzema and Gareth Bale wasn't going to be easy—or so they thought. In reality, Manchester City blew their opponents out of the water with a 4-1 victory. While Phil impressed spectators, it was his friend Díaz who stole the headlines. The young Spaniard scored City's

fourth goal with a thunderous strike from outside of the box. Manchester City's youngsters weren't just there to watch—they were determined to show that they were the stars of the future.

Their final match of the tournament was in Nashville against Tottenham Hotspur. Manchester City defeated their opponents 3-0 and put on a strong performance for their American fans to enjoy. John Stones, Sterling and Díaz all scored.

Phil and his academy teammates had come to the USA as new starters in the senior squad. As young players

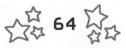

given the opportunity of a lifetime, they had grabbed it with both hands. Phil had given Guardiola some serious thinking to do. After a remarkable pre-season, was Phil ready for the jump up to first-team soccer?

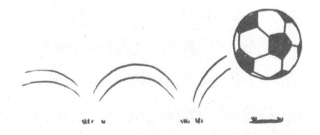

PLAYER
OF THE
TOURNAMENT

Outside of the club, Phil's talents
had not gone unnoticed. He had
often been invited to play for the
England youth sides, giving him an
opportunity to team up with the very

best players around his age. In 2017, Phil was picked as a member of the England squad to play in the U17 World Cup. Taking his skills to an international stage once again, Phil joined his teammates on a flight to India.

Phil woke up on the plane to the sound of laughter. As he opened his eyes, he saw a phone light flash in front of him.

"Got you, sleepyhead," said Sancho with a grin.

Although Sancho was leaving Manchester City, he had been called

up for the international tournament too. The pair sat next to each other on the plane.

"Can't catch a minute's rest around you," Phil muttered.

After a long flight, the England squad arrived in Kolkata. They headed to their training base and started to prepare for group matches against Chile, Mexico and Iraq. Phil and Sancho weren't the only exciting prospects in the team. The U17 squad also included Emile Smith-Rowe, Callum Hudson-Odoi, Marc Guehi, Morgan Gibbs-White and Rhian

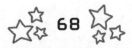

Brewster. This was a talented squad more than capable of returning home with winner's medals and a trophy.

The group stage could hardly have gone any better for The Three Lions. They thrashed Chile 4-0 in their opening game before defeating Mexico 3-2 and Iraq 4-0. Phil and Sancho both scored in the win against Mexico.

The locals were fully embracing the tournament and most matches had 50,000+ fans in attendance. It was by far the largest crowd many of the young players had played in front of. It gave

the tournament a real buzz, much like the senior World Cup.

Having progressed from the group stage with the maximum points available, England headed into the knockout stages with confidence. Their opponents in the round of 16 were Japan, who held England to a 0-0 draw after full time and extra time. With neither side able to grab a winner, this meant that penalties were needed.

Phil volunteered to be England's third penalty taker. He stepped up to the penalty spot. Although he was getting used to the Indian heat, nothing could stop him sweating at that moment. The Japanese goalkeeper stood tall and the thousands of fans around the stadium watched Phil's every move. Phil ran up to the ball and hit it as hard as he could. *Goal!* Phil had scored his penalty. All he could do now was hope his remaining teammates did the same.

England were victorious in the penalty shootout with a score of 5-3. All five England players scored their penalties. England progressed to the quarterfinals, where they defeated the USA 1-4. They then went on to beat

Brazil 1-3 in the semifinal, setting up a final against Spain.

Not too long before the U17 World Cup, Phil had taken part in the U17 European Championships. England had made it all the way to the final of that competition, too, but had lost the match on penalties to Spain. This time around, Phil was determined not to let that happen.

The game did not start as planned. Within the opening half an hour, Spain scored twice, giving them an impressive lead. But with plenty of time still to play, England began to step it up. In the 44th minute, they found a way back into the match when Brewster scored a header. After scoring, he ran into the goal to pick up the ball and sprinted back to the center circle. There was no time to be wasted.

In the second half, England brought the game level. Gibbs-White scored from close range. The score was 2-2 and the teams were evenly matched. That was until Phil showed the thousands in attendance just what he could do. Hudson-Odoi sprinted down the left wing and crossed the ball. Phil ran onto it and fired it over the

diving goalkeeper. *Goal!* It was 3-2 and England had fought their way back. But could they hold onto their lead?

In the 84th minute, Guehi latched on to a loose ball to double England's advantage. This made the score 4-2 with only a handful of minutes left to play. But Phil was not done just yet. In the 88th minute, he ran into the opposition box and struck the ball with his weaker right foot. The ball powered across the ground and snuck beneath the goalkeeper. *Goal!* It was 5-2 and Phil had grabbed himself a brace.

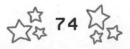

There were no longer any ifs or buts. The U17 World Cup belonged to England! As the referee brought the game to an end, Phil and his teammates celebrated on the field. The team lined up to receive their winner's medals and then lifted the trophy in front of thousands of excited fans.

In recognition of his performance across the tournament, Phil was awarded the Golden Ball. This was the award given to the best player of the entire tournament. Everyone at Manchester City knew just how talented Phil was. Without a shadow of a doubt, he was a rising star. And now the entire soccer world was excited to see what this talented youngster could become.

8
SILVA'S SHADOW

On his return to Manchester, Phil was invited to Guardiola's office. It was his first day back at the training complex and coaches and teammates welcomed him back into the academy with congratulations for his Golden Ball. Phil opened the door to the manager's

office, where Guardiola waited behind a large desk. Pictures of Guardiola's soccer playing days hung on the walls and a smaller frame of his family rested on the desk. But the most interesting sight was standing to the right of the manager. It was the attacking midfielder David Silva. Guardiola grinned at Phil's confusion.

"Welcome back," said Guardiola, rising from his seat and shaking Phil's hand.

"Nice to meet you," said Silva.

"Yeah, great to meet you too!" said Phil, taking a seat and trying to hide his excitement. As Silva also took a seat by the desk, Phil pinched the skin on his right arm to check he wasn't dreaming.

"You were fantastic in the tournament," said Guardiola.

"Thanks, coach," said Phil.

"Although, on behalf of us Spaniards … don't do that to us again," laughed Guardiola.

"I can't make any promises," laughed Phil.

"I like your confidence," said Guardiola. The manager leaned forward, clasping his hands together, with his elbows resting on the desk. "You both must be wondering why

you're here. Well, firstly, Phil—not only were you brilliant in the tournament, but you were great in our pre-season friendlies in the USA. I was very impressed. I don't just want you to play with the first team every once in a while. I believe you're ready to practice with them every week."

Phil's eyes lit up at the news. "That would be an honor!" he said. "I won't let you down."

"I'm certain you won't," said Guardiola. "David, I'd like you to take Phil under your wing. Teach him everything you know."

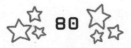

"I will, boss," said Silva. "But I'm not ready to give up my spot in the team just yet!" he joked.

Day after day, Phil followed Silva everywhere. He shadowed when Silva trained in the morning, and he monitored how the Spaniard fueled himself at meal times. Phil wanted to soak up every bit of information he could. David Silva was a Manchester  City legend. He'd given everything to the club and had played a crucial role in turning the side into title challengers.

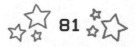

Silva was similar to Phil in size. He, too, was a smaller player with an incredible awareness of his surroundings. He was able to easily duck and dive in between rushing defenders and marching midfielders. He was always in control of the ball and two steps ahead of anyone else on the field.

Steadily, Phil's game started to improve. Impressed by Phil's development, Guardiola included him in the matchday squad for a Champions League match. Manchester

City were playing against Dutch side Feyenoord Rotterdam at home, during the tournament's group stage. Manchester City had all but wrapped up progression from the group stages, but they still wanted to win in front of their home supporters.

With fifteen minutes to go in the match, Guardiola signalled Phil to get up off the bench. So far neither side had been able to break the deadlock and the score remained 0-0.

"You'll change the game for us," Guardiola winked. "Congratulations Phil."

Phil replaced Yaya Touré and was welcomed onto the field by thousands of clapping hands and cheering voices. The fans knew that he was one of their own: a local lad, living the soccer dream. Could he play his part in a victory?

With only a couple of minutes left in the match, Phil ran to the left wing, stretching the Feyenoord defenders across the line. Gündoğan played a through ball to Sterling on the right-hand wing. With the Feyenoord defense stretched, Sterling burst into the box and took a shot. He pulled

back his right foot and struck the ball into the back of the net.

Phil ran over to his teammates to celebrate. The team kept their lead, and Phil tasted victory on his first ever competitive match as a Manchester City player. As the thousands of fans stood up and roared for their team, Phil stood in the middle of the field with his hands on his hips. It had happened. He'd done it. He wasn't the young boy sitting in that stand watching his heroes. He was now one of the eleven on the field. And to some young fans

in the crowd, he was becoming their hero, too.

Phil continued to learn and progress within the team. With such a talented squad, match time in the Premier League was hard to come by. However, Guardiola gave Phil his chance in cup competitions. On the 25th of September 2018, Phil enjoyed a match to remember. It was a third-round League Cup tie away to Oxford United. With Oxford being in the third league of English soccer, it was not a match to get fans excited. But this didn't matter to Phil. It was a match

where he was given an opportunity to shine, and he sure took it.

Manchester City defeated their opponents 0-3, and Phil stole the show. The young attacker assisted the team's second goal, sending a delicate through ball for Riyad Mahrez to slot past the advancing goalkeeper.

In the 92nd minute, with the game all but won, Sterling played the ball to Phil inside the box. Phil brought it under his control and fired it at goal from the left. It rifled past the goalkeeper and struck the back of the net.

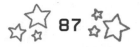 87

Although it had little impact on the game, Phil celebrated as if he'd scored the winner in a cup final. This was his first ever goal for the Manchester City first team, and it was a feeling that he'd never forget. He couldn't wait to experience such a moment again. It was only a cup tie against weaker opposition, but match by match and minute after minute, Phil was showing just what he was about.

In a team stacked with multimillion dollar talents, many would have written off Phil's chances from the start. But this local lad from Stockport

was here to stay. Among the well-
known names and high-profile stars
was a talent from City's very own
academy. Here was a player who
did not look out of place among the
world's best.

9

WORLD DOMINATION

At the point that Phil joined up with the first team, Manchester City were an unstoppable force. They fired their way to titles and trophies galore. However, for Phil it felt like he hadn't earned the trophies himself. While he had been able to break into the odd cup game,

he still hadn't gotten a regular starting
spot in the Manchester City lineup. He
was proud of the small parts he had
played over a two-year period. But part
of him felt that these trophies weren't
actually his.

One day after training at the start
of the 2019/2020 pre-season, Phil
snuck off to the club's trophy room. He
walked along the glass cabinets
examining the trophies
City had won. Some were
from before he was born
and some even before his
parents had been born!

It was as he made his way to the recent trophies that memories started to come back to him.

First he saw the 2018 League Cup. Manchester City had defeated Arsenal at Wembley 0-3, with goals from Agüero, Kompany and Silva. In the final minute of that match, Phil was substituted onto the field to replace the tired Agüero. He could almost hear the booming applause as Agüero was given a standing ovation by the crowd.

Not too far away was the 2019 League Cup trophy. Manchester City had won that particular competition

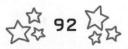

two years in a row. Phil greatly appreciated this trophy. Out of all the competitions won, this was the one he had played in the most. He featured in every round of the competition up until the cup final where he was on the bench. Manchester City defeated Chelsea on penalties in the final and claimed the cup.

Next up was the 2019 FA Cup. But Phil didn't have too many fond memories with this trophy. He hadn't even been included in the matchday squad for the final, when City defeated Watford 6-0.

Front and center were Manchester City's Premier League trophies. There was the one that they had won during the 2017/2018 season. Phil hadn't even played half a match during this campaign, so it certainly didn't feel like his trophy. But there were happy memories of being in and around the squad during a title-winning campaign. He proudly remembered training every day with determined winners.

Then there was the club's most recent achievement: the 2018/2019 Premier League trophy. This one felt better, with Phil having made thirteen appearances during the season. But it would have felt amazing if he'd played in every match. It was in this campaign that Phil had scored his first Premier League goal. It was a match-winner in front of a max-capacity crowd at the Etihad stadium, against Tottenham Hotspur. The three points won here were crucial, as Manchester City were being chased all the way by Liverpool. At the end of the season, Manchester

City were able to go just one point better than their rivals and hold on to their Premier League crown.

As Phil admired the trophies, the lights in the room went out. Phil chuckled to himself in the darkness. It was getting so late that even the cleaners were getting ready to go home. When Phil pulled his phone from his pocket and saw the time, his eyes widened. He switched on the phone light and darted for the door. Trophies and medals were not the only important things in Phil's life now. Recent events ensured that he'd not

only grown up as a soccer player but he'd grown up as a person too. In early 2019, Phil had become a parent.

10
FATHERHOOD

On the 22nd of January 2019, midway through the Premier League season, Phil was as tense as if he were playing in a high-stakes match. He was sitting on a hospital chair outside of a delivery ward, watching the seconds tick by on a clock.

"You can come in now, Mr. Foden,"

called the midwife. "Or should I say 'daddy'?"

Phil entered the hospital room with a massive smile, and there they were. Phil's girlfriend, Rebecca, was holding their child. A baby boy was resting against her chest, and Phil was overwhelmed with emotion as he approached the bed.

"I'm so proud of you," said Phil, hugging Rebecca. "You did so well."

"These nine months haven't been easy," she said, smiling. "But worth every minute."

The pair of them looked at their newborn son, his eyes closed, chest rising steadily, tiny fingers curled up.

"Welcome to the world, Ronnie," Phil whispered, stroking the baby's head.

Being under the spotlight at Manchester City had helped Phil to grow up fast, but this was something entirely different. Becoming a father at the age of 18 meant that Phil had to grow up even faster. He was now responsible for another human being.

 Nurturing Ronnie became Phil's motivation. No matter whether he won or

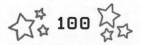

lost a soccer game, he always had his responsibilities at home.

Six months after Ronnie was born, the 2019/2020 Premier League season got underway. While 2019 had been huge for the Foden family, it was also a big year for Phil on the field. David Silva was playing in the last year of his contract at Manchester City. All signs pointed to him leaving the club at the end of the 2019/2020 season. That meant a spot would be open in the team. In preparation for this, Phil earned a lot more game minutes during the season. However, this

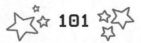

season was less successful than the previous two.

Manchester City were unable to win a third Premier League title in a row. Instead, the title headed to Anfield— an unstoppable Liverpool team proving to be the best that season. Despite not winning the Premier League, the year was not without trophies for Manchester City. Phil helped his side to another EFL Cup triumph, making it three years in a row that the club had won the competition.

At the end of the campaign, Manchester City legend David Silva confirmed that he was leaving the club that he had spent ten years with. He was an iconic player who Phil and thousands of fans idolized. Silva was certainly going to be missed, but the club had a ready-made replacement with Phil. Could Phil be the player to help his side reclaim their Premier League crown?

11
LEADING MAN

In the 2020/2021 Premier League season, Phil was no longer a bench option, but a player who deserved first-team minutes. His time had come. Guardiola knew that it was time to unleash Phil on the main stage.

Phil started the season exactly as he'd hoped. In a match against

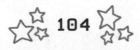

Wolverhampton Wanderers, Phil marked his intent for the campaign. After a flurry of passes, Sterling darted into the left side of the penalty area. He looked up and saw Phil charging into the box. Sterling passed the ball and Phil fired it into the net. *Goal!* Manchester City won their opening match of the season 1-3 and sent out a warning to their rivals: they wanted their title back.

But the next handful of games did not go as expected. Defeats to Leicester City and Tottenham Hotspur, as well as draws with Leeds United,

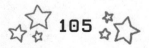

West Ham and Liverpool had fans questioning whether Manchester City had what it took to win the league. Those doubts turned out to be misplaced.

With a talented side including Phil, a rising star hitting the form of his life, Manchester City turned the tables and went on an incredible run. The team were unbeaten for nineteen games in the league. This included big wins against Chelsea and Liverpool. It was their city rivals, Manchester United, who ended the league streak.

Manchester City were beaten 0-2 at their home ground, the Etihad Stadium.

This defeat did not undo all of the great work that the team had put in before it. Manchester City steamrolled their way to yet another Premier League triumph. They finished the season with a comfortable gap of twelve points between them and the closest challenger.

Phil played in over twenty-eight matches in the league during the season and was an important attacker for the team. He held his own among

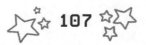

 an attacking squad that contained the likes of De Bruyne, Sterling, Mahrez and Bernardo Silva. Phil scored nine goals and provided five assists during the campaign.

On the final day of the season, with the trophy already won, Phil and his teammates put on an incredible performance for the home fans in attendance. Fans were gradually being eased back into stadiums following the COVID-19 pandemic, and a lucky few thousand were able to celebrate with their heroes.

Phil scored in a 5-0 victory against Everton. As the final whistle blew, Phil dashed over to the fans and applauded them from the field. He searched through the blur of celebrating fans and found the seats that he and his mom had sat in all those years ago. His mind flashed back to when Agüero had scored that wondergoal and won the title in the 2011/2012 season.

But now it was Phil's moment. He'd achieved his dream and had led his team to Premier League glory. As Phil gazed into the crowd, a hand landed on his shoulder. Agüero, the

hero in that momentous 2012 victory, was standing side-by-side with Phil. It was Agüero's final Premier League appearance before moving to Barcelona. Phil joined the City fans around the stadium in giving him a standing ovation.

★ ★ ★

A few days after the victory, Phil returned to the club's trophy room. Proudly displayed in the center was the club's latest addition: the 2020/2021 Premier League trophy.

If previous trophies had felt undeserved, the same could not be said about this one. Phil had earned the right to be known as a Premier League champion. On the form that he had shown, there was even a chance that he was going to be called up to the England squad for Euro 2020. Could Phil become an international champion before the year was out?

12

EURO 2020

Phil's rise at Manchester City came with extra attention. His talent could not be ignored after putting in dazzling performances every week. It wasn't long before England manager Gareth Southgate rewarded Phil with his first ever cap in a match against Iceland. As Phil's performances in the

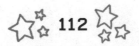

league were only getting stronger, Southgate continued to call Phil up to England squads for friendlies, qualifying matches and Nations League fixtures.

But England had a wealth of talent in attacking midfield. Jack Grealish, Mason Mount, James Maddison and Jesse Lingard were all competing for a place in the squad. With such depth of talent available, was Phil going to be one of the players picked to play at Euro 2020?

Southgate selected a squad of thirty-three players to train before he made his final decision. Phil was one of those players. But the excitement didn't end there, as Phil's England teammates and the media alike were in for a surprise when Phil turned up to his first training session.

"Are you sure you want to do this?" said Phil's hairdresser.

"Positive," said Phil. "I want something fresh and exciting."

The hairdresser got to work on Phil's hair. He had the same haircut he

 always had: closely shaven, neat and stylish. But this time there was an added

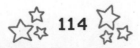

twist—Phil had decided to bleach his hair blonde!

"Say hello to the new Phil Foden," said the hairdresser, holding up a mirror.

Phil's new hair color took everyone by such surprise that it was the main topic of conversation for a couple of days. Many people compared him to Paul "Gazza" Gascoigne—a famous former England international who scored an incredible volley against

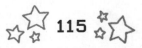

Scotland at Euro 96. Phil didn't mind the odd joke or reference to Gascoigne. He had changed his hair to feel his best, and to perform with confidence and swagger.

Phil's time training with England went by in a flash. Soon it was decision time. After one of the sessions, Southgate asked Phil if he'd like to go for a walk around the training field.

"I'm just going to get straight to it," said Southgate. "I've been really impressed with what I've seen from you during the season and when

you've trained with us here. I want that grit, determination and talent in this side. How's that sound?"

"Amazing!" said Phil. He'd just been selected to play for his country in a major international tournament. He'd watched his heroes play in World Cups and Euros since he was a little boy. Now he was going to be one of the players proudly wearing The Three Lions badge for the senior team.

Southgate had been so impressed with Phil's training that he selected Phil for the team's opening group

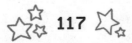

stage match against Croatia. Phil started the game fiercely. His determination created an early chance, but his shot fired against the post. The thousands of England fans inside Wembley Stadium were about to jump out of their seats and celebrate, but instead let out a sigh of disappointment. Phil played well through the rest of the game, and thanks to a goal from his City teammate Sterling, England won the match 1-0.

This performance put England on course for an incredible tournament.

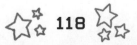

A draw against Scotland, plus victories against Croatia and Czech Republic sent England through to the knockout rounds. They then defeated Germany, Ukraine and Denmark in their run to the final. For the first time in years, England made it all the way to an international final.

England were in touching distance of the trophy, but standing in their way were a gifted Italian side. In the build-up to the final, the players

 trained as hard as they could to earn a first-team spot. Phil gave

his all during every session, to put himself in with a change of making the starting eleven for the final. But during one session he pushed himself *too* hard. Phil picked up a knock during training. No matter how hard Phil pushed, he couldn't get past the pain, and he knew he wouldn't be able to perform at his best.

Although England had made it all

the way to the final, Phil knew that his part on the field was over. Despite this Phil remained upbeat,

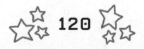

supporting his teammates from the sideline and wishing them the best.

After a night full of twists and turns, England and Italy had to settle the match with a penalty shoot-out. Five brave lions volunteered to take penalties for England: Harry Kane, Harry Maguire, Rashford, Sancho and Bukayo Saka. However, thanks to incredible saves from the Italian goalkeeper, Gianluigi Donnarumma, Italy won the penalty shoot-out.

Although England had not won the trophy, the team had made themselves incredibly proud. With a young, hungry team and players such as Phil who would only get better with experience, things were looking up for this England side.

13
ROAD TO QATAR 2022

The knock that kept Phil out of the
Euro 2020 final turned out to be more
serious than first thought. Following
medical scans, it was discovered
that Phil had injured his foot. He
had to wear a protective boot and
use crutches. So instead of running

across training fields, scoring goals and celebrating wildly, it was time for stillness. Phil was to stay at home with family and enjoy a well-deserved rest. At least that was the idea ...

Phil was sitting in his garden, soaking up the summer sun with his family surrounding him. His son, now two years old, was sitting on the grass.

"Play soccer," said Ronnie, pointing at a ball.

"I can't," said Phil, pointing to his foot. "Daddy's hurt his foot."

Ronnie's eyes started to water and he opened his mouth ready to cry. Before

he could, Phil gave in.

"Okay, okay," said Phil. "But we have to be careful."

Phil took his crutches off the table and hobbled over to his son.

Ronnie was dressed the part. He was wearing a child's Manchester City top, and to him this garden was as important as the Etihad Stadium. Phil got the ball and placed it on an imaginary penalty spot. With his two crutches keeping him upright, he stood in front of the small soccer goal in his garden.

"Are you ready?" asked Phil.

Ronnie nodded, concentrating as hard as he could. He took two steps forward, poking his foot out and kicking the ball. It slowly rolled toward the goal. It was heading for the bottom corner. On his crutches, Phil was rooted to the spot. Had Ronnie hit it hard enough? The ball looked like it was losing speed, but it was so close. It made it all the way to the goal line, but could it cross it? *Yes!*

"Gooooal!" said Phil.

Ronnie smiled and lifted his arms into the air.

"Gooooooal!" Ronnie cried, copying his father.

Phil had changed so much—from the young boy playing on the streets outside of his family home to the academy prospect fighting year after year to make it for his boyhood club. Despite the doubts and obstacles, he'd become a star in his own right within a club filled with talent. Not only had he broken into the first team, but he had helped them be crowned as the champions of the Premier League. Still only at the start of his career, Phil's trophy cabinet is sure to grow.

Phil is an amazing soccer player. And no matter where his career takes him, he'll keep playing with the same childlike wonder that made him fall in love with soccer on those Stockport streets years ago.